MICHAEL J. FOX

by
Jill C. Wheeler

A&D
BIOGRAPHIES
Star Tracks

Visit us at
www.abdopub.com

Published by ABDO Publishing Company, 4940 Viking Drive, Edina, MN 55435. Copyright ©2001 by Abdo Consulting Group, Inc. International copyrights reserved in all countries. No part of this book may be reproduced in any form without written permission from the publisher.

Printed in the United States.

Graphic Design: John Hamilton
Cover Design: MacLean Tuminelly
Cover photo: Shooting Stars
Interior photos:
  Amblin Entertainment, Universal Pictures, p. 24, 26, 38
  AP/Wide World, p. 10, 11, 17, 19, 28, 33, 36, 39, 50, 51, 54, 56, 59
  Corbis, p. 5, 6, 9, 12, 15, 21, 23, 25, 27, 31, 35, 41, 43, 44, 46, 47, 53, 57, 60-61, 63
  Shooting Stars, p. 45, 49
  Time Pix, p. 37, 55

Library of Congress Cataloging-in-Publication Data
Wheeler, Jill C., 1964-
   Michael J. Fox / Jill C. Wheeler.
      p. cm. — (Star tracks)
   Includes index.
   ISBN 1-57765-551-6
      1. Fox, Michael J., 1961—Juvenile literature. 2. Actors—Canada—Biography—Juvenile literature. 3. Actors—United States—Biography—Juvenile literature. [1. Fox, Michael J., 1961- 2. Actors and actresses.] I. Title. II. Series

PN2308.F69 W48 2001
791.43'028'092—dc21
[B]

                                                  00-069989

CONTENTS

THEY'RE JUST MOVIES

ON SEPTEMBER 22, 1982, MANY AMERICANS tuned in to a new television show. *Family Ties* told the story of Steven and Elyse Keaton and their four children. The Keatons had been hippies when they were younger. They wanted to pass those same values on to their children, yet it didn't always work.

The Keaton's oldest son, Alex, was different. He was a loyal Republican and believed in capitalism instead of activism. He always wore suits and ties. He even read *The Wall Street Journal,* though he was only in high school. Beneath the conservative exterior, Alex P. Keaton had a heart of gold. Viewers could tell he loved his family even though their opinions differed.

Michael has never been one to let success go to his head.

Family Ties fans quickly grew to love Alex P. Keaton. They also wondered about the sandy-haired, blue-eyed young man who played him. Who was this newcomer? Before long, they were sending about 500 fan letters a week to the young actor.

The actor was 21-year-old Michael J. Fox. He would be the star of *Family Ties* for the show's seven-year run. He would win three Emmy Awards for his portrayal of Alex. And he would go on to a successful movie career.

Michael's life has been full of surprises—both good and bad. Throughout, he's kept a positive attitude. He's never been one to let his success go to his head. "You constantly have to come back to the truth that you're just a guy… like everybody else," he said in a magazine interview. "You can… love something like acting, because it's a valuable and worthwhile craft… but it's not brain surgery. They're just movies."

CANADIAN

E X P O R T

FOX WAS BORN MICHAEL ANDREW FOX on June 9, 1961, in Edmonton, Alberta, Canada. He changed his middle initial from "A" to "J" when he started acting. He didn't want people to think he believed he was "Michael, A Fox."

His father, William (Bill), was a Canadian army officer for 25 years. Bill's work took the family to different Army bases all over Canada. When Bill's time in the army was up, the family settled in a suburb of Vancouver, British Columbia. All the traveling had made Michael, 11, very close to his three sisters and his brother.

Michael always was one of the shortest kids in his class. His father was only 5-feet, 6-inches tall, and had once been a jockey. His mother, Phyllis, was a mere five feet tall. When he was young, Michael read that eating more could help a person grow. He began eating a lot, but it only made him grow out—not up. At one time he weighed about 140 pounds. "I used to look like a pasta salesman," he joked.

One of Michael's heroes was actor Jimmy Cagney. Cagney also was short. He starred in many movies in the 1930s. His quick wit kept people laughing. Michael took a cue from Cagney and made up for his height with extra charm and confidence. He didn't let it stop him from doing what he loved. In his case, that was ice hockey.

Like many Canadians, Michael loved playing hockey. As a boy he wanted to be a professional hockey player. He played aggressively and fearlessly. He made both the PeeWee and Junior leagues.

Michael has had some 56 stitches in his face because of sports and an active youth.

*Michael skating at a
charity hockey match
between the Hollywood
All-Stars and Boston
Bruins alumni.*

Hockey is a tough sport with many injuries.
More than once, Michael's face got beaten during
the game. He also ripped his nose open falling
from his bunk bed when he was 10 years old and
cracked a tooth playing roller hockey. All in all,
he had some 56 stitches in his face.

"I always wanted to do something in the arts."

Michael was only 4-feet, 9-inches tall when he turned 14. The other hockey players were much bigger and getting taller all the time. Michael quit hockey and took up playing the guitar. At one time he made a few dollars singing and playing. He also loved writing stories. "I always wanted to do something in the arts," he said. "I was determined to be a musician or a writer or an artist or an actor."

Yet even playing in a band didn't seem to work when it came to getting a girlfriend. Michael's mother remembers that he spent a lot of time with girls, but he always said they were just friends. Finally he announced to his parents that he was joining a drama club to meet girls. His plan backfired. Instead of getting hooked on a girl, he got hooked on acting.

THE
SMALL
SCREEN

WHEN HE WAS 15, A TEACHER TOLD Michael about an opening in a Canadian Broadcasting Company (CBC) show called *Leo and Me*. The part was that of a bright 10-year-old boy. Michael always had looked young for his age. Still, he was surprised when he passed the audition and got the part.

"It didn't seem like a big deal," he recalls. "I never had any idea like, 'This is it! I'm a star!' I just thought it was interesting to be on TV." He quickly learned to love the work and dropped out of high school so he could put more time toward acting. (In 1995, he finally would earn his high school diploma.)

Leo and Me aired for two years. Michael followed that up with more radio and stage work, including the play *Shadow Box*. It was then that he decided to make a career in the entertainment industry. While his family was supportive, they didn't really believe their son would do it. Except perhaps, his grandmother.

"My mother used to worry because I was always small for my age and I acted so crazy at times," Michael said. "But my grandmother always said, 'Don't worry, he'll get through it, and then he'll be famous someday.'" It was his grandmother who told his mother not to worry when Michael dropped out of school to pursue acting.

Shortly after *Shadow Box*, Michael met some people who already were famous. He played the grandson of actors Art Carney and Maureen Stapleton in a TV movie filmed in Vancouver. The movie was called *Letters from Frank*. The two veteran actors were impressed with Michael's abilities. They encouraged him to move to Hollywood and try to land more acting jobs.

Michael thought long and hard about their suggestion. It was scary, and he knew he would miss his family. Yet he couldn't pass up the opportunity. He sold his guitar for extra cash, and in June 1979, his father drove him to Los Angeles. Michael had just turned 18 years old.

"Leaving everything behind to start a whole new life at such a young age may seem brave," he later said. "But the truth is I just wasn't mature enough to realize there were risks involved."

"My mother used to worry because I was always small for my age and I acted so crazy at times."

THE
BIG
BREAK

IN HOLLYWOOD, MICHAEL BEGAN competing with hundreds of other young actors for parts in movies and on TV shows. He had a role in the 1980 movie *Midnight Madness*, and then landed a role in a CBS TV series called *Palmerstown USA*. Michael beat out 300 other actors to star in *Palmerstown*, a drama set during the Depression. Critics liked the show, which ran for two years.

He followed that up with guest appearances on a number of TV shows, including *Lou Grant* and *Trapper John, M.D*. Then he did another movie, *Class of '84,* in 1982. The movie was a violent story of drugs and gangs set in a Los Angeles school. Many countries banned the movie because it was so violent.

Michael on the set of Family Ties.

After *Class of '84*, things began to change. Michael would go to auditions and read well, yet he wasn't called back. When he asked why, he was told he was either too short, or that he looked too young. His debts grew and he started selling off his furniture so he could buy food.

Meanwhile, he knew he couldn't make himself taller. However, at 140 pounds, he could make himself slimmer. He went on a crash diet, eating virtually nothing but macaroni and cheese. He lost 20 pounds and his image seemed to change.

Michael was just about ready to head home to Canada when his agent called. He said there was a new TV comedy looking for a young actor to portray the teenage son. Michael hesitated. He didn't want to play teenagers all his life. Nor was he sure he wanted to take on a role in a comedy. He'd never done comedy, and he felt his older brother was better at being funny than he was. Still, it was a job, and he needed that. He agreed to audition for the part of Alex P. Keaton.

In Hollywood, Michael began competing with hundreds of other young actors.

Michael was so eager at his first audition that he didn't do a good job. Gary Goldberg, the producer of *Family Ties*, wasn't impressed with Michael's first audition. But the casting director was. She thought Michael was perfect for the part. She pressed Goldberg to let Michael try a second time. He did. The rest is history.

When Michael began *Family Ties*, he was living with a roommate in a one-room apartment. He was too poor to own a car. His *Family Ties* co-star, Meredith Baxter Birney, would pick him up in the morning and give him a ride to the studio. "My roommate saw this beautiful blonde in a Mercedes with a sunroof picking me up every day and figured I had it made," Michael said. He only wished his grandmother had lived long enough to see him in the show and realize that her faith in him had paid off.

In 1986, Betty White and Michael J. Fox posed with their Emmy Awards for Outstanding Lead Actress and Actor in a Comedy Series. White won for her role on The Golden Girls *and Fox for his on* Family Ties.

BACK
TO THE
FUTURE

WHEN *FAMILY TIES* ESTABLISHED MICHAEL
as a promising young performer, additional offers
came pouring in. He landed appearances on *The
Love Boat*, *Night Court,* and *Battle of the Network
Stars*. He starred in the made-for-TV-movie *High
School USA* with Nancy McKeon of *The Facts of
Life*. He starred again with McKeon in the TV movie
Poison Ivy. Gossip columnists speculated that

Michael and Nancy were dating.
Family Ties made Michael J.
Fox a household name around the
world. But it wasn't until 1985 that
he became a superstar. Two
Michael J. Fox movies hit the
theaters that year: *Teen Wolf* and
the spectacularly successful *Back to
the Future*.

Back to the Future

Back to the Future was the story of young Marty McFly, who travels back to the 1950s to help his parents fall in love. The somewhat strange Doc Brown, played by Christopher Lloyd, helps Marty. The movie's producers initially wanted Eric Stoltz to star as Marty. However, they realized he wasn't quite right. They needed an actor with vulnerability and youthfulness. They found just what they were looking for in Michael.

Doing both *Back to the Future* and *Family Ties* made for long days for Michael. For three months in early 1985, he would work on *Family Ties* from 10 a.m. to 6 p.m., then work on the movie from 6:30 p.m. to 2:30 a.m. On Fridays, he would tape *Family Ties* until early evening, then report to the movie set and work there from 10 p.m. to 6 or 7 the next morning.

Back to the Future

Michael performs a stunt on the set of Spin City.

Back to the Future was the biggest hit of the summer of 1985. Michael's efforts garnered him a number of awards, including Most Exciting New Star of 1985, given by the National Association of Theater Owners. His new fame even allowed him to meet Princess Diana and then-President Ronald Reagan.

Back to the Future made even more people tune in to *Family Ties*. During the '85-'86 season, *Family Ties* was second only to *The Cosby Show* in attracting viewers. During that season, viewers met a new character. Her name was Ellen Reed, Alex P. Keaton's first girlfriend. A young actress named Tracy Pollan played Ellen.

For his work in television and cinema, Michael was named Most Exciting New Star of 1985.

MR. MOVIES

BETWEEN A TV SERIES AND MAKING movies, Michael spent most of his time working. When he did have free time, he enjoyed going back to Canada to visit his family. He also enjoyed playing guitar, reading horror stories, exercising, and listening to music. He had a chance to play guitar and sing in his next movie, *Light of Day*. He starred with rock star Joan Jett. The movie was not successful, but Michael's star barely flickered.

That same year, movie fans saw Michael in *The Secret of My Success*. It was a romantic comedy about a farm boy from Kansas who goes to work in New York City. He ends up pretending to be someone he's not. After the movie, gossip columnists said Michael was dating his co-star, Helen Slater.

Michael with rock star Joan Jett.

Michael was linked to many women during his early years in show business. He learned to take it in stride. He realized it would be tough going for any woman who dated him. "You meet someone, you have to say to her, '…your picture is going to be in 90 magazines…'" he said.

Following *The Secret of My Success*, Michael returned in a dramatic role in *Bright Lights, Big City*. Once again, he played a young man in New York City who runs into trouble with drugs and nightclubs. The film also featured Tracy Pollan in a small part. Pollan had played Michael's girlfriend on *Family Ties* a few years before.

"Michael was linked to many women during his early years in show business."

*Michael J. Fox and his wife Tracy Pollan arrive at
the 52nd Annual Primetime Emmy Awards,
September 10, 2000. Michael won the Emmy for
Outstanding Actor for his work in* Spin City.

Michael J. Fox and Tracy Pollan.

Both Michael and Tracy had been seeing other people when they worked together on the TV show. Things were different now. Michael took advantage of that to ask her out. "It sounds really horrible, but it was one of those things," he said. "Someone goes, 'Did you hear that so-and-so aren't together anymore?' You go, 'Hmm, that's too bad. Where's the phone?'"

Seven months after they began dating, Michael proposed. It was December 1987. Shortly after they made their engagement public, bad things began to happen. Michael was in Thailand filming a new movie, *Casualties of War*. While he was gone, Tracy began getting scary letters. The letters threatened to kill her and Michael unless they ended their engagement. Over the course of a year, they received more than 5,000 threatening letters.

Seven months after he and Tracy began dating, Michael proposed.

Michael and Tracy went to the police. An investigation revealed that a 26-year-old woman was sending the letters. A court ordered her to stop bothering the couple. Michael also hired a security consultant to keep him and Tracy safe.

Michael J. Fox and his wife Tracy Pollan arrive at the 56th annual Golden Globes in Beverly Hills, California, January 24, 1999. Michael won for best actor in a television comedy series.

Michael and Tracy at a Hollywood dinner party.

Michael and Tracy were married on Saturday, July 16, 1988, at a country inn in Arlington, Vermont. They kept the details of the ceremony a secret until the end. Security guards patrolled the nearby woods to catch any uninvited guests. Their efforts still couldn't stop helicopters carrying photographers from circling over the inn. The noise of the helicopters nearly drowned out the voices of the wedding party.

People later asked Michael whether the helicopter noise had bothered him. He said no. *Casualties of War* had featured many scenes with helicopters. Michael was used to the noise by then.

BACK-TO-BACK
FUTURES

BACK TO THE FUTURE HAD BEEN SUCH A huge hit that people began talking about a sequel almost immediately. In fact, Michael ended up shooting two sequels. *Back to the Future II* hit movie theaters in 1989. *Back to the Future III* was released in 1990.

The second sequel had Marty McFly traveling into the future to help his son. Then he had to return to 1955 to stop his enemy, Biff, from changing the future. The third sequel sent Marty back to the old West to rescue Doc Brown. There they met Marty's great-great grandparents.

Back to the Future III

Michael J. Fox and his Back to the Future co-star Lea Thompson at the 1997 People's Choice Awards.

Michael filmed the first sequel while still doing *Family Ties*. To make matters more complicated, Tracy was pregnant. She gave birth to their first child, Sam Michael Fox, while Michael was filming *Back to the Future II*.

Fortunately for Michael, *Family Ties* ended its run before he had to shoot *Back to the Future III*. The show that had made him a star had lasted seven years. That made things a little easier. Yet he also received the news that his father, William, had died while he was filming the second sequel.

Michael himself had a near-death experience during the shoot. In *Back to the Future III*, like in many of his movies, he did his own stunts. He nearly died when a hanging stunt went wrong. The crew thought he was doing a great job of pretending to be strangled. Then he passed out and everyone realized it was real. A doctor on the set revived him.

Michael J. Fox holds hands with his wife, Tracy Pollan, and their son, Sam, at the 1995 Kids for Kids benefit in New York City.

SPIN CITY

MICHAEL'S MOVIE CAREER TOOK A
negative turn after the two sequels. He starred in a
series of films that didn't do well at the box office.
They included *The Hard Way*, *Doc Hollywood*,
Life with Mikey, *Where the Rivers Flow North*,
For Love or Money, *Greedy*, and *Coldblooded*.
Michael was disappointed with the movies as well.
"I felt really frustrated and unhappy," he said. "I
was making movies… which were driven by the
idea that they'd make lots of money. Nobody
cared about character or script. Only how big
they'd open."

Beyond movies, Michael was trying his hand
at several new things. He hosted an episode of the
NBC late-night comedy *Saturday Night Live*. He
directed and starred in a short on *Tales from the
Crypt*. He provided the voice for several children's
movies. He hosted a tribute to his own childhood
hero, Jimmy Cagney. And like many celebrities,
he starred in commercials for companies like Pepsi
and McDonald's.

Michael J. Fox with his wife, Tracy Pollan.

Things began to change for the better in 1995. He landed a part in the successful film, *The American President*. Even though the part was small, Michael showed he still had talent. Even more importantly to Michael, 1995 saw new additions to his and Tracy's family. They welcomed twin girls, Aquinnah Kathleen and Schuyler Frances, on February 15, 1995.

In March 1996, he was asked to star in another TV comedy series. It was called *Spin City*. The writer was Michael's former *Family Ties* producer. Michael would play the role of the deputy mayor of New York City. He also would co-executive produce the series.

Michael performs a stunt on the set of Spin City.

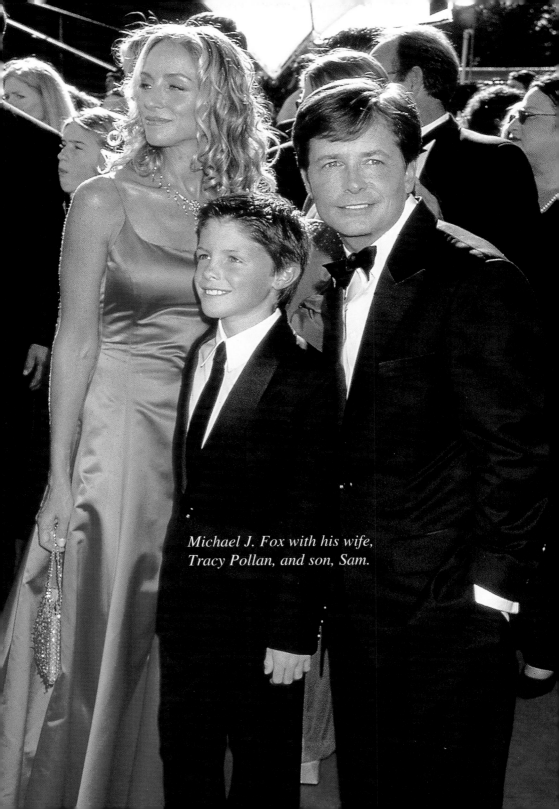

*Michael J. Fox with his wife,
Tracy Pollan, and son, Sam.*

Spin City debuted in September 1996. The show was a hit and quickly made it into the top 10 TV shows. In addition to *Spin City*, Michael found time to do a TV special with his actress wife. The rest of the time, the family of five was happy at home in Manhattan or in their country home in Connecticut.

To the outside world, it appeared as though the short kid from Canada had the perfect life. In a few years, all that would change.

Michael J. Fox poses with his Screen Actors Guild Award, which he won at the 6th Annual Screen Actors Guild Awards March 12, 2000, in Los Angeles. Michael won for his work in Spin City.

Michael with Spin City co-star Heather Locklear.

TREMORS
AND
SHADOWS

WHILE FILMING *DOC HOLLYWOOD* IN 1991, Michael noticed a twitching in the little finger of his left hand. Six months later, the tremor had spread to much of his left hand. His shoulder also had become achy and stiff. He decided to see a doctor. The doctor ran some tests. Then he told Michael he had Parkinson's disease. Michael couldn't believe it.

Parkinson's disease is a neurological disorder that causes people to lose control of their physical movements. No one is exactly sure what causes it. It usually strikes older people. Michael was only in his early 30s.

Both Michael and Tracy were shocked. Michael recalls when he told his wife. "Neither of us quite understood," he said. "We hugged each other and assured ourselves that we'd be able to deal with it." They also decided to spread the news only to their closest friends and family.

As time passed, Michael's whole left side was affected. Even his young son noticed the tremors. "We had a whole routine where he'd pump my hand," Michael said. "That kept it still for three or four seconds." Michael continued to see doctors, but no one seemed able to help. Michael learned many little tricks to hide his condition from the public.

Michael J. Fox holds his award for outstanding lead actor in a comedy series for his work in Spin City *at the 52nd Annual Primetime Emmy Awards in Los Angeles, September 10, 2000.*

Michael on the set of Late Night with David Letterman.

Finally, he turned to medication. The drugs would still some of the tremors, yet they took a while to take effect. Michael would take them only before he had to appear in public or give an interview. He recalls waiting backstage before going on *Late Night with David Letterman*. He was praying his arms would stop trembling before he had to go on stage. "When I went out, everything was fine," he said. "But as I sat there having a conversation, I was thinking, 'You don't know the game I just played.'"

At the Golden Globe Awards in January 1998, Michael's body was shaking so much he couldn't get out of the limousine. He had to have the driver go around the block while Tracy massaged his muscles. "He probably thought I was nuts," Michael said of the driver. "But I just couldn't get out of the car and let my arm go, or mumble, or shuffle." That night he picked up the Golden Globe for Best Actor in a Comedy for his work on *Spin City*.

A few years before, Michael had heard about a new brain surgery for Parkinson's victims. The operation was usually successful. However, there was a chance the patient would die or end up paralyzed if something went wrong. Michael decided to take the chance and have the surgery. He waited until he had finished the second season of *Spin City*. Then he told his cast mates about his disease and said he was having surgery.

Michael was awake during the surgery. He recalls how strange it was to think that the surgeon was inside his head. "They did something once that slurred my speech, and I thought, 'Oh man, you're messing with my brain. It's freaking me out.'"

Michael J. Fox holds his award for Best Performance By An Actor in a Television Series for his role in **Spin City** *during the 57th annual Golden Globe Awards, January 23, 2000, in Beverly Hills, California.*

NO MORE

SECRETS

THE SURGERY WAS A SUCCESS. IT STOPPED the worst of Michael's tremors. Having told his cast mates, it also eased his stress on the *Spin City* set. Now people understood when he couldn't do all the stunts he used to do. They understood if he needed to wait a few minutes before shooting while his tremors quieted.

Few people outside the set knew what challenges Michael faced each day. Just before Thanksgiving 1998, Michael decided to tell the rest of the world. He was doing the voice for the title character in *Stuart Little* at the time. Even the director of that movie was surprised when he heard the news. Michael handled the news, and the many questions afterwards, with his usual professionalism. And his sense of humor.

"I love the irony," he said. "I'm perceived as being really young, and yet I have the clinical condition of an old man." Almost immediately fans began sending him cards and well wishes. Many people thought he was a hero for speaking up.

Stuart Little

NEW ROLE FOR MICHAEL

IN JANUARY 2000, MICHAEL ANNOUNCED that he was leaving *Spin City*. He said he wanted to have more time to spend with his family. He also said he had a new mission: helping raise money to find a cure for Parkinson's disease.

Just days later, he picked up his third Golden Globe for his performance on *Spin City*. As he accepted the award, he joked, "Actor out of work! News at 11!" Then he walked into Tracy's waiting arms offstage, and began to cry.

Michael credits Tracy for helping him make it through these tough times. People close to the couple say their troubles have made their marriage that much stronger.

Michael speaking in Washington, D.C.

On September 28, 1999, Michael J. Fox spoke in front of a U.S. Senate committee in Washington, D.C. The committee was holding hearings for research and treatments for Parkinson's Disease.

The road ahead is equally long and hard. Michael summed it up when he testified before members of the United States Congress. He was there to ask them to allocate more money for research to find a cure for Parkinson's disease.

"I can still perform my job… help out with the daily tasks and rituals involved in home life," he told them. "But I don't kid myself. That will change. I can expect in my 40s to face challenges most wouldn't expect until their 70s or 80s," he said.

Michael says he believes researchers will find a cure for Parkinson's. He's optimistic that could happen in as few as 10 years. For now, he's taking things one day at a time.

"It's made me stronger," he says of his disease. "A million times wiser. And more compassionate. I've realized I'm vulnerable, that no matter how many awards I'm given or how big my bank account is, I can be messed with like that.

"I feel good and I'm happy and I have energy and there's stuff to do."

Michael J. Fox walks off the stage holding up his Emmy for best actor in a comedy series for his work on Spin City *at the 52nd Annual Primetime Emmy Awards, September 10, 2000.*

Michael J. Fox at the 52nd annual Emmy Awards, September 10, 2000. Fox won Outstanding Lead Actor in a Comedy Series for his role in Spin City.

WHERE ON THE WEB?

You can find out more about Michael J. Fox by visiting the following web sites.

Filo Fox: The Official Michael J. Fox Fan Club
http://members.aol.com/FiloFox/

The Michael J. Fox Encyclopedia
http://www.bttf.com/fox.htm

Michael J. Fox Page
http://members.aol.com/mjfxpage/mjfox.htm

A Place for Michael J. Fox
http://www.geocities.com/TelevisionCity/Stage/
2006/

Fans also can write to Michael at:
Michael J. Fox
c/o Creative Artists Agency
9830 Wilshire Boulevard
Beverly Hills, California 90212

GLOSSARY

Hippie: a young person who doesn't believe in established codes of behavior.

Neurological disorder: a disease involving the central nervous system.

Parkinson's disease: a disease that makes it harder and harder for a person to control his or her muscles.

Michael speaks in front of a U.S. Senate committee investigating Parkinson's disease.

INDEX